How to Prompt Better

# How to Prompt Better

–

## A Beginner's Guide to Working with AI

Niklas Drude

## Imprint

Author:

Niklas Drude
c/o Postflex #3055
Emsdettener Str. 10
48268 Greven
Germany

contact@niklasdrude.com

Editor:
Clara Abigail

Fonts:
Merriweather, Raleway & Passion One
from Google Fonts

ISBN: 9798856858913
Independently published.

# Contents

# Introduction

I don't want you to spend your time or money on something that does not provide you with value. So, this introductory section is meant to help you decide whether this book is for you.

If you are reading this only after purchasing the book: well, tough luck. I do hope that this book will still meet your expectations and that it will propel your prompting skills to the next level. Feel free to skip ahead to the section titled "General Advice."

## What is this book about?

As you might have guessed from the title, this book aims to advise beginners on how to write better prompts for generative AI.

Generative AI is artificial intelligence that creates stuff – like images, texts, code, or even music. A prompt is an instruction you write to let the respective AI know what you want it to create for you. The better you become at writing these prompts in a way the AI understands, the better the AI's outputs will align with your expectations. Thus, if you want to improve the quality of an AI's outputs, you should enhance the quality of your inputs.

This book will help you with precisely that. It will aid you in understanding what differentiates a good prompt from a bad prompt and how you can improve your prompts, regardless of the type of AI you are working with.

# Do you need prior knowledge?

You do not need to know anything about artificial intelligence to benefit from reading this book. Actually, quite the opposite is true: the more you don't know about AI and prompting, the more you can learn from this book.

By now, you probably have heard quite a bit about artificial intelligence in the news. You may have already given generative AI a try yourself and played around with a couple of prompts, but you may feel like you don't yet get the results you want or that you see others achieve.

Does this sound like you? Then you are exactly the kind of person I had in mind when writing this book.

If you are not a techie, don't worry. I won't go into the technical details of how AI models work. After all, even to their creators, AIs are black boxes in many ways. While they know how and on what kind of data their AIs have been trained, they usually cannot explain the reasoning of an AI that has led to a specific output.

That technical knowledge is mostly irrelevant for writing great prompts for existing AIs – just like you don't need to understand the circuitry on the board of your smartphone to send a message. If you are no stranger to using computers or smartphones, you should not have problems understanding this book.

Depending on your level of experience with prompting AI, you might consider the first few pieces of advice to be commonplace remarks. But trust me, they are only if you have already worked a bit with AI in the past. I have personally introduced multiple people to working with AI and had to learn myself that it is best not to expect any prior knowledge. And since this book is meant to be a beginner's guide, it's essential to ease newbies into the world of AI, which to some may seem intimidating at first glance.

But even if you are an advanced user – good for you! – you might find some advice helpful. Some suggestions might inspire new ideas for great prompts. Some recommendations might provide reasoning to your gut feeling for effective prompting. Or, at the very least, you will find yourself affirmed in already doing everything right – which is a nice feeling anyway.

## Will this book teach you about a specific AI?

The AI space is growing and evolving at a rapid pace. Yet I am convinced that we are, at the moment, only witnessing the beginning of an exponential development. Consequently, I expect to see significant advances in AI technology being made at an ever-increasing rate in the future.

We have already seen previously established leaders in their respective fields of AI being overthrown in a matter of days by newly released models that surpass their predecessors' capabilities and seemingly come out of nowhere. This is likely going to happen again and again for the foreseeable future.

Additionally, the existing AI models get frequent updates and, accordingly, get equipped with new features. This opens entirely new use cases but also comes with additional ways of writing prompts for the respective AI.

Consequently, any book focusing on specific AI tools risks being outdated within weeks of publication. And I want your learnings from this book to stay relevant for longer than the next month.

I firmly believe that in the ever faster-spinning world of AI, your time is better spent learning the underlying basics of prompting than reading (and probably forgetting) prompt hacks for a specific AI. While that might be a shortcut to re-ceiving decent outputs, you would remain reliant on exter-nal help whenever you want to work with a new AI or ap-proach new use cases.

So, instead of giving you a fancy list of prompts, which you could copy-paste for a specific AI, this book will instead equip you with the knowledge to write your own prompts for any use case and for any AI working with text prompts. Instead of trying to convince you to use a specific AI (with respective affiliate links attached), this book will try its best to improve your prompting skills for the long term.

Even if you later look into tool-specific publications, which I would not necessarily discourage, the knowledge you have gained from this book will help you understand why the given example prompts in those publications work well. Or you might even get ideas on how to improve those prompts further.

All advice in this book has been written to be as future-proof as possible in this quickly evolving field so that you will hopefully benefit from reading this for years to come.

## Was this book written by AI?

Since this book is about working with generative AI, I would not blame you for assuming that I might have had an AI write this entire book for me. After all, there are quite a few books out there on this topic, which presumably have been entirely created by AI, judging by their style of writing. And it's easy to see why.

With the right prompt, you can have a text-generating AI come up with pages worth of written content within minutes instead of going through the lengthy process of writing yourself. This makes it very tempting to throw together a few AI outputs and call it a book and a day.

Considering this, you might be surprised to hear that I wrote this entire book myself. This is for two main reasons.

At the time of writing this, text-generating AIs tend to have a cutoff date for their training data, which lies well in the past. Meaning that, ironically, the AI itself would not know about the most recent developments in the space of AI. To a certain degree, this may be remedied by working with AIs that have unrestricted access to the Internet. But this comes with the risk that the AI would just regurgitate the thoughts and ideas of blog posts, potentially written by AI.

But most importantly, the world does not need yet another AI-written book about AI. There are already enough, and there will be even more in the future. When a lot of "authors" write similar prompts to have the same AI, which is currently leading in its segment, generate a book about the same topic, you would expect the results to be more or less alike.

And as Albert Einstein may or may not have said, "Insanity is doing the same thing over and over again and expecting different results." From what I have seen so far, many of the resulting books feel more like a generic and relatively shallow top-ten listicle blog post, inflated by repetition to the length of a book. My intention was to provide you with more value than that. Plus, I wanted to sprinkle in a few anecdotes here and there to make the advice more memorable. So, if you are looking for a soulless AI-written book on AI – I'm sorry, you won't find it here.

I did, however, enlist a couple of AIs to aid me in creating this book. And I would like to give credit where credit is due.

When I was dissatisfied with a few sentences but simply could not convince my brain to spit out the phrasing I was looking for in a timely manner, I asked the AI tool Jasper for help. While Jasper is capable of writing entire texts, I only worked with it to rephrase a couple of sentences. With Jasper, I could quickly go through dozens of different versions of the same sentence within minutes; I only had to pick my favorite.

In the fast-moving world of AI, spending hours to fine-tune each sentence of a book about prompting is simply not an option. I would have risked this book to be already outdated upon publication. Thus, Jasper was a great help to speed things up when encountering a mental roadblock. However, I only used its support sparsely, as I felt like it intercepted my writing flow when I was consulting it more frequently in the beginning. Since *perfect* is the greatest enemy of *done*, I decided to stop optimizing every other sentence and to be satisfied with *good enough*. After all, I did not write this book to win any literature awards but rather to pass on my experience.

Furthermore, I wanted this beginner's guide to be as complete as possible. To ensure I do not forget anything important, I decided to interview an AI on how it would like to be prompted. Thus, I also asked ChatGPT for advice to write better prompts to see whether I had forgotten any essential aspects. And while most pieces of advice from ChatGPT's output were already on my list for this book, there were still a few things I might have missed otherwise. And likewise, there were many tricks missing in ChatGPT's output, which were already on my list, which reinforced my sentiment that writing the book myself was a good idea.

For the book cover design, I already had a certain style and a couple of specific ideas in mind. So, I had Midjourney create a couple of first drafts for me. I then picked my favorite of those designs and used it as a reference when creating the cover design by hand with vector graphics.

And finally, I used Grammarly to comb through my text and iron out the worst typos and imperfections before I handed the manuscript over to my human editor. (Thanks a lot, Clara for doing an amazing job!)

All of this is also meant to illustrate my stance on current AI technology: for now, AI is not a cure-all in my eyes. At the time of writing, we should not entirely rely on AI to do all of our work for us. Instead, I believe that we receive the best results if we integrate artificial intelligence deliberately and purposefully into our workflows so that AI and us humans can both play to our strengths.

# General Advice

The first piece of advice: don't skip this section because you are interested in only one specific type of AI. This part of the book is probably even more relevant to you – even if you plan to use only one kind of AI – as it contains the essential knowledge to write better prompts in *any* type of generative AI.

# 1 Know What You Want

Ideally, after reading this book, your prompts will lead the respective AI to create outputs that will meet or even exceed your expectations. But for this to work, you'll need to have expectations in the first place. As a consequence, knowing precisely what you want the AI to generate for you is the first crucial step. Otherwise, you will have a hard time verbalizing your intention into a prompt to the AI.

We probably all have been in a situation where a friend of yours was hungry and wanted to go and get something to eat with you. But they did not know what or where they would like to eat. So, you made a couple of suggestions, yet your friend did not like any of them. Don't be that friend — neither in real life nor in when prompting an AI.

If, for example, you ask an image-generating AI to create "a nice picture," this description would fit a romantic photo of a sundown below palm trees on a tropical beach or a cartoon drawing of a cute kitten. Playing around and finding out what the AI would consider to be "nice" can be exciting and fun in itself. However, if you need the generated results for a specific use case, make sure to think about what you want before trying to tell the AI.

# 2 Choose the Right AI

Another reason why it is important to know what you want is that it allows you to pick the AI best suited for the job. (Don't worry, we will get to prompting soon enough).

Not all AIs are created equal. At the time of writing this, there is no artificial *general* intelligence (yet) that can adapt to any situation and thus help you with any request. Different AIs have been trained to take on different tasks and to excel in different scenarios.

While this might seem like a no-brainer, it is not. Sure, I probably don't have to tell you that you should not ask a text-generating AI to create a video for you. Even though it could generate ideas for the plot of a video or even scripts for entire movies, it would not be able to output a video file for you. But oftentimes, there are different AIs, which technically could do the same job, but would give you different results.

While one image-generating AI might be best at creating photorealistic pictures that can hardly be distinguished from the works of a professional photographer, another AI might excel at creating artistically impressive illustrations. Just like you would not go to just any doctor for any medical procedure (your dentist probably is not the best qualified to give you a colonoscopy), you should not just pick any image-generating AI to create a picture for you.

But it does not stop there. Many AI tools provide you with different models to use. Some might be more advanced than others. But they are often just trained on different sets of data so that they outperform each other at different tasks.

This plethora of AI models may seem intimidating at first. And to be honest, that does not really change since new AI models get released all the time. But there is a myriad of YouTube videos discussing which AI and which recent model is best suited for which use case, usually comparing results side by side. So, you don't have to test everything yourself but can first take a look at the opinions of other, more experienced users to get a head start.

Also, you can find (mostly) friendly communities on Reddit and Discord to ask any question you have. Most users there will be more than happy to show off their expertise. Just make sure you don't ask the exact same question that gets asked almost hourly. This could – understandably – result in annoyed responses. So, use the respective platforms' search to check whether a similar question has already been asked in the past. This way, you might not even have to wait for an answer.

But back to the topic. Make sure you find the AI model which best suits your needs before you start thinking about your prompts. This might take a bit of time, but it is well worth it. The quality of your results is always capped by the capabilities of the respective AI model in that use case – regardless of your proficiency at prompting. And you want this cap to be as high as possible for your specific needs.

Now let's finally look into the actual prompting.

# 3 Be Clear and Concise

This is easily the most widespread piece of advice when it comes to writing better prompts. You will probably find it in every single blog post on prompting. If you have already consulted other sources to learn more about this topic, it is virtually impossible not to have come across this exact phrase. And this is for a reason: it is important.

So, at the risk of boring you, for the sake of completeness, let me elaborate on this. We are going to get to the good stuff soon – pinky promise.

If you want to get the AI to do what you want it to do, it first must be able to understand what you want. In this regard, AIs are no different from human contractors or employees, as they also must know what you want in order to fulfill your request.

If you have ever worked with somebody else, you will probably have had the experience that lousy communication leads to bad results. Consider prompting as a way of communicating with artificial intelligence. AIs are getting increasingly smarter and, in some regards, already surpass the capabilities of their human counterparts. Because of this, even bad prompts may generate surprisingly competent outputs. But even if those outputs are not necessarily bad, for the foreseeable future, one thing will remain true: better communication leads to better results.

As you will realize over the following chapters, many of the pieces of advice given to improve your prompts will, as an added benefit, also improve your inter-human communication skills. Or viewed from the opposite perspective, if you write your prompts to be as easily comprehensible to other humans as possible, chances are you will also improve your prompts to be more understandable to AI. And one of the most important things to make your communication more intelligible is – you guessed it – to be clear and concise.

Many of the following pieces of advice will help you achieve exactly that and will go into much more detail. But let me touch on what it means to be clear and concise.

Try to distill the essence of your prompt and cut away any unnecessary padding. Sure, it is essential to tell the AI everything it needs to know to fulfill your prompt properly. But feel free to remove any redundant or irrelevant information.

Also, the longer a sentence gets, the more complex its structure becomes and the harder it becomes to understand. I know that I'm anything but innocent in this regard. And I am tempted to blame it on being from Germany. We love using extensive multi-clause sentences and absurdly long words like the infamous "Eierschalensollbruchstellenverursacher" (a term for a punch-bell egg cracker). But to be fair to my fellow German citizens – most people would probably just call it an "Eiöffner" ("egg-opener").

I have digressed pretty far from the actual topic. Avoid doing that while prompting. This way, your prompts become clearer and more concise.

# 4 Avoid Ambiguity

A bat can be a flying mammal or a wooden club used to play baseball. A bass can be a type of guitar or a fish. A metal fan might love a certain music genre or help ventilate the room. These are just a few examples of lexical ambiguities. They do a great job of confusing AIs. Imagine prompting an AI to create a picture of "a bat with a bass and a metal fan." Good luck trying to get the AI to generate exactly what you intended.

What makes it especially difficult for the AI to understand what you mean is the lack of any context. While "a baseball player swinging his bat" still is not entirely unambiguous, the AI can infer what kind of bat you meant from your provided context. Because it – most likely – has not been trained on any images of baseball players swinging around poor nocturnal animals, it will most certainly have the player wield a wooden club (which, by the way, is also an ambiguous term).

So, unless you really want a bass guitar to swim in the ocean, problems resulting from ambiguity can often be mitigated by providing context.

However, lexical ambiguity is not the only kind of ambiguity that might pose a challenge when prompting AIs. There is also syntactic ambiguity.

Here is an example: *The neighbors exercised too much with their dogs. And then they died.*

This definitely is a tragic story with at least two casualties. But who exactly died here? The neighbors, their dogs, or all of them? This is a rather considerable difference.

If you don't want the AI to kill off the wrong guys in your text, it helps to be aware of potential sources of ambiguity and avoid it wherever possible.

# 5 Check Your Grammar and Spelling

Have you ever read a comment on the internet with such horrible spelling that you simply could not understand what its author was trying to communicate? If not, you probably do not spend much time online, or you only frequent the most highly cultivated communities the interwebs have to offer.

What hinders communication between humans makes it even more difficult to convey meaning to an AI. While we humans often do not even notice minor typos, AI models have been trained to draw connections between certain strings of letters.

While AI will vastly improve over time to understand the meaning of words from their context, even with the wrong spelling, there may be circumstances when the misspelling creates a new word, which would also make sense in the respective context – e.g., *cat* instead of *hat*. Or there might not be any context to learn anything from to begin with.

My personal favorite example of a misspelling dates back to an era when there were no smartphones. Whenever you wanted to write someone a message on the go, you had to use SMS. Since most phones did not have full keyboards, you had to use the number buttons to write letters as well. Each button was associated with three to four letters of the alphabet. By pressing a button multiple times, you could cycle through the respective letters. This was a very slow way of writing.

A system called "T9" (short for "text on nine keys") made this process quite a bit faster. You only had to press each button once, and the phone would guess which word you wanted to type. This caused many funny hiccups in communication, as people started to rely more and more on T9 and did not always check their messages after writing to see whether the intended words had been picked by T9.

Now to the actual anecdote: I don't know whether this has actually happened or belongs in the realm of urban legends, but it does not matter to bring across my point. One of my high school friends told me that one of his friends once received an invitation via SMS to come to a party. What he meant to text in response was: "Great, I'll bring beer." What he actually responded was: "Great, I'll bring AIDS."

Needless to say, his response first raised a few eyebrows and then the corners of a few mouths.

(Just to stop a few self-proclaimed myth-busters in their tracks: this story happened in Germany. And in German, the same combination of numbers was used to write B-I-E-R and A-I-D-S, which was 2-4-3-7. Also, you could legally buy beer at the age of sixteen).

Today, the struggles with T9 are a thing of the past for most people. They have been replaced with a fight against auto-correct, which has drastically improved over the last few years with the rise of machine learning. Still, we are not immune to typos. Thus, it makes sense to check your spelling and grammar before submitting a prompt. After all, you would expect quite different outputs when asking an AI about beer or about AIDS.

If this example is too exaggerated for you, here is another one. In most countries, students write tests, and their performance gets graded. However, there are different grading systems. One such system uses the letters from A to F. Another system uses the numerals from 1 to 6. Which system do you prefer? The letter or the latter? By changing a single alphabetic character, you can turn the meaning of the entire statement into the exact opposite. And it certainly does not help that *letter* and *latter* are pronounced similarly.

Don't even get me started on "your" and "you're." Talking about "your food" and saying "you're food" have entirely different meanings – at least for everyone with a non-cannibalistic diet. And while AI will undoubtedly evolve to compensate for our inability to write with proper spelling, it's best to avoid any misunderstanding in the making.

Another important aspect of grammar and spelling that is often overlooked is punctuation. We often think of commas, periods, and semicolons as expendable. After all, spoken language also gets along without pronouncing punctuation marks. However, we use intonation and pauses to structure sentences in a way that brings across the intended meaning. In writing, these cues are missing. We need punctuation as a replacement.

Punctuation (or the lack thereof) can completely change the meaning of a sentence. Here is an example: "Let's eat kids!" Eating infants is quite morbid, right? What if I add a comma? "Let's eat, kids!" The sentence immediately become much more wholesome. Punctuation can save lives!

Now you might argue that this is an artificially construed example designed to be as drastic as possible (and to cause a few chuckles). And I would agree. However, there are situations when missing punctuation may cause problems in real life. Here is an example from my personal experience.

I once took a scientific test to see if I had ADHD (which I don't). The test consisted of many statements I had to rate based on how much they applied to me on a scale from "not at all" to "very much." The problem was, while these statements contained enumerations of traits, they did not have any commas.

One item, in particular, caused me a bit of trouble. I should decide whether I was "acting without thinking impulsive." As I do not think impulsively at all when acting, I very much agreed with this statement. I understood "impulsive" as a flat adverb like in "think positive."

The authors, however, had intended to affix "impulsive" as an additional trait. With correct punctuation, the statement should have read "acting without thinking, impulsive." This is the exact opposite of what I understood. Consequently, I ticked the precise opposite of what I should have ticked on the scale.

I was still pretty far away from the threshold score at which you would consider someone to have ADHD. So, in my case, this did not make much of a difference. But for other people with fringe cases, this misunderstanding might have caused them to be falsely diagnosed with ADHD and even be put on medications that they did not need or that might cause harm in the worst case.

Spelling and punctuation matter. While all of these little anecdotes do not have anything to do with AI, they illustrate how improper orthography may lead to potentially fatal misunderstandings. AIs have been trained to be prompted with human language. In general, this makes communicating with AIs much more intuitive. But it also introduces many problems with inter-human communication into the process of working with AI. So, make sure to watch your spelling, or else the AI might bring AIDS instead of beer to your outputs.

# 6 Review Your Prompts Before Submitting

Checking your own prompts also helps iron out any potential orthographic shortcomings. But there are also other reasons why it makes sense to review your inputs before you press the submit button.

First of all, if you are anything like me, your thoughts might be racing faster than you can write while conceptualizing the prompt, making it easy to forget something you wanted to include in your prompt. When proofreading your own input, you might realize that you only thought about adding something to the prompt but did not actually write it. This happens to me more often than I like to admit.

Rereading the prompt allows you to check whether the prompt is comprehensible. Try to read the text from the perspective of the AI. Is any information missing that might help the AI fulfill its task? Does the prompt contain any potentially problematic ambiguity? And most importantly, is it clear what you want the AI to do?

And finally, reviewing the prompt gives you another opportunity to remember the advice from this book and adjust your input accordingly.

# 7 Break Complex Prompts into Smaller Parts

Could you draw a stick figure with a pen you hold with your mouth, balance a glass of water on your head, write a blog post on your laptop, tell a child a bedtime story, all while standing on a single leg? To most people, none of these tasks would be impossible to complete when they can be handled one by one. However, when all of them have to be done simultaneously, they probably would not stand a chance. Complexity creates difficulty. (In case you want to give it a try anyways, make sure to send me a video!)

We are really bad at multitasking, especially when asked to perform contrary tasks at the same time. You probably know the coordination exercise, in which you should rub your belly in a circular motion while patting yourself on the head with the other hand, moving your hand up and down. This may sound easy, but it is surprisingly tricky. If you don't believe me, give it a try. You will probably need to focus quite a bit to execute both motions flawlessly. Even tasks with a relatively low level of complexity may become challenging when they contain opposing or seemingly contradictory aspects. Contrariety also creates difficulty.

Both of these insights can be applied to AI, as well.

When you ask the AI to perform a particularly complex task, it might struggle. For instance, this might be the case when you request an AI to create an image containing a large amount of individually described objects – e.g., "a banana, an apple, two oranges, a peach, five strawberries, and a bunch of grapes in a wooden bowl next to a honeydew melon on a marble table in a Mediterranean landscape." In this case, the definition of specific positions and amounts of fruits add an additional level of complexity. At the time of writing, you would end up with a bowl of rather funny-looking fruits.

Likewise, if you ask the AI to create something with contra-dictory or physically impossible aspects, it might have trouble producing your desired output. Think of prompting an AI to create an image of an igloo in the desert or a poem about a horse riding itself while the sun shines bright at night. (Though, in these examples, some degree of weird-ness in the output might even be desirable.)

If the AI repeatedly struggles to create outputs that live up to your expectations, your prompt might be too complex or contain confounding elements. In these cases, it might help to break up your prompt into discrete parts and reassemble the separate outputs later on.

Just like in the earlier examples, it's often not the individual elements of a prompt that make it difficult to fulfill, but ra-ther the simultaneous combination of them.

# 8 Prompt in English

If you know English, which I would assume you do since you are currently reading this book in that language, you should write your prompts to AIs in English, too, whenever the language of the output is irrelevant.

AIs are getting better and better at understanding prompts in different languages. Yet I expect AIs to generate better outputs when prompted in English for quite some time. This has three reasons:

A vast majority of the internet is in English. According to W3Techs, almost 55% of all analyzed websites used English as a content language in 2023, followed far behind by Spanish with 5%. Since English is the lingua franca of the internet and the World Wide Web is an easily accessible source of all sorts of data, I would be surprised if English wasn't the dominant language in the training data of most AIs.

Many of the leading companies in the field of AI are based in English-speaking countries. This adds further bias toward using English training data. While I would not completely rule out that egocentrism might play a small role as well, most notably, the creators of an AI need to be able to test the quality of the AI's outputs before releasing it to the public, and this is much easier when prompting in your native language.

Many of the most lucrative markets are English-speaking. At this point, the United States of America still has the largest economy in the world. According to data from the World

Bank, the US accounted for almost a quarter of global GDP in 2021. When including India (rank 5), the UK (rank 6), Canada (rank 9), and Australia (rank 13), these five countries add up to more than a third of the global economy. Furthermore, if you also consider all the ventures and free-lancers worldwide that want to do business with companies in these lucrative markets and thus profit from AIs that work with English inputs and outputs, it becomes apparent that first optimizing your AI for the English language makes the most sense.

The same also applies to outputs of text-generating AIs; they tend to be of higher quality when generated in English. In case you do not require the output to be in a specific language, you should go with English. (If you write your prompt in English, the result will most likely automatically be in English.)

I have caught AIs multiple times conceiving text outputs in English first and then translating them later to the desired output language. One thing I always like to try when testing new text-generating AI models is to ask the AI to come up with jokes in different languages, as humor is something AIs have struggled with for quite some time. Usually, the AI then tries to generate some short puns. But rather often, they are not funny at all in non-English output languages. This is especially true for homophonic puns.

Here's a quick example: Why can't a bicycle stand on its own? Because it has two wheels. That isn't funny at all? Well, how about this: Why can't a bicycle stand on its own? Because it is two-tired. When the AI only translates the literal meaning of the words, the actual payoff of the joke – "two-tired" being phonetically similar to "too tired" – is lost.

On another occasion, I wanted to copy a generated German text for later use by clicking on the AI's provided "add to clipboard" button. Interestingly, when I pasted the text into a document, the entire text was in English. This suggests that the text was indeed first generated in English and then only translated to German on the surface of the user interface.

As AI models get better at understanding and reproducing language, the differences in quality between languages will diminish over time. However, if you want to get the most out of an AI, you will probably still get the best results when using English prompts for the foreseeable future.

Please note that there are also AIs that have been explicitly trained to work with a specific language. It goes without saying that this advice does not apply to those AIs.

# 9  Know the Limitations

Maybe even more important than knowing what an AI excels at is knowing in which fields an AI is terrible. As I explained in the chapter "Choose the Right AI," not all AIs are created equal. If you know what the specific AI – or artificial intelligence in general for now – cannot accomplish, you will know when it is time to take the results from one AI and feed them into another one or when you should even continue to work manually from there on.

There may be an AI that generates the best images but does not have any inpainting features (inpainting allows you to select an area of an image in which an AI should generate something new). Another AI might only be trained on data up to a specific year and thus cannot know about things that happened afterward.

The problem with the limitations of an AI model is that they are not featured prominently in its marketing material. You will probably have to dig through blog posts, news articles, or online communities to find proper information about the AI model's shortcomings.

When testing an AI yourself, try challenging it with especially complicated cases to see how it performs. If you only ever write prompts that play into the strengths of the AI (pretty much any image-generating AI can create a picture of a cat), you will never learn about the AI's limitations. This might cause you to trust in the quality of the outputs of the AI, even in cases when you really shouldn't.

But please consider these snapshots of the technology's current limitations to be temporary. It is more than likely that many of these shortcomings won't stay there for long with AI technology improving faster and faster. Thus, don't completely write off an AI because it cannot do a certain thing. It might learn to do that in the near future.

# 10  Use AI-Specific Commands and Parameters

For the most part, many AIs have learned to understand human language. This way, you can simply write your prompt in English, and the AI will know what you want it to do. However, there are some instances in which AIs come with their own set of additional commands and parameters, which allow you to specify how the AI should interpret your prompt or let you do things more efficiently.

Thus, it makes sense to read through the AI's documentation, user manual, or readme file – whatever it may be called. Even though you certainly won't remember all available commands and parameters the first time you read through them, it is helpful to keep in the back of your mind that a certain functionality exists in case you should ever need to use it. When the time comes, you can then consult the documentation again.

For example, if you want the AI to create multiple outputs for the same prompt, you do not necessarily have to copy and paste the prompt time and time again. There might be a parameter that lets you specify how often you would like the AI to repeat the prompt for you. This can save you quite a lot of time.

Usually, AIs have their most recent model active by default. However, there may be some cases in which you might want to return to an older model – e.g. if you would like to create more in the style of your previous outputs. There might be a command or a parameter that allows you to specify which model to use.

Certain parameters may allow you to specify technical settings for your output, like aspect ratios of images. You might be able to ask the AI to open your usage statistics or even access otherwise completely hidden features. Also, you may be able to define a section of your prompt containing negative prompts, which brings me to my next piece of advice.

# 11 Use Negative Prompts

Negativity has a bad reputation. When we talk about something negative, we usually think of something we would rather avoid. This, however, is not the case when it comes to AI; in prompts, negativity is a positive thing.

Oftentimes, you get to your desired output much faster and easier by not only letting the AI know what you want but also what you don't want, and this is what negative prompts are for.

Let's say you want the AI to generate an image of a street in downtown New York City. Even though you did not tell the AI anything about cars driving on this street, the AI might be inclined to add them itself, as it has learned from its training data that the streets of downtown New York tend to be filled with cars.

If you want the street to be completely empty, you would probably intuitively add the word "empty" to the prompt, which definitely is not a bad idea. But if the AI has rarely, if ever, seen a street without any cars in downtown NYC, the AI might believe the vehicles to be an inherent feature of New York City's downtown streets (and thus even include them on "empty streets"). In this case, it might help to tell the AI explicitly that you want no cars in your image with a negative prompt.

Not all AIs have dedicated input fields, commands, or parameters that allow you to input negative prompts. But you can still try to add a "no cars" or "without cars" after your positive prompt and see if the AI understands that you don't want any cars in the output.

# 12  Specify the Desired Format or Media Type

Many AIs allow you to choose different formats and types of media for your output. Let's say you prompt an AI to create a text about the perfect vacation. It could generate a blog post for a travel blog writing about a fantastic journey to exciting destinations. Or it could write a list of the ten things you should pack into your luggage for a perfect vacation. It could also generate a social media post, a novel outline, a movie script, etc. There are many different ways to create texts about the exact same topic.

So, it makes sense to let the AI know which kind of text you want to create. Otherwise, the AI will either tend to lean towards the type of writing that was most prominent in its training data, or it will produce a rather generic text that is not optimized for any specific use. Needless to say, the text will most likely be more effective in reaching your goal if you allow the AI to tailor it to the intended use.

Even if you do not plan to use the text itself, e.g. if you only need the generated ideas contained in the text, it makes sense to define an output format that makes it faster and easier for you to absorb the relevant information. Would you rather go through a neat list of all relevant thoughts or read through a lengthy encyclopedia entry?

So far, we have only looked at text AIs in terms of output media types. But this also applies to many different kinds of generative AIs. When working with image-generating AIs, you can tell the AI whether the output should look like a photo, an illustration, or a computer rendering. Furthermore, you can often choose the aspect ratio or the image's resolution. Some image-generating AIs can also output the generation process as a video file – but only if you ask it to do so.

When you work with AI to create music, you may be able to pick a genre, the length of the desired piece, the rhythm, and the output file format.

(On a side note: always go with uncompressed WAV files if you can when choosing an audio output format. They might be larger than MP3s or AACs. But they will retain all information about the analog audio signal and thus sound much better to audiophiles. This is very helpful if you want to (use an AI to) master the track later on, as this might bring out frequencies that were previously almost inaudible and thus were heavily compressed. And if you want to sell the generated music online, some platforms only accept WAV files because of their higher audio quality.)

But you are not limited to setting technical details for your outputs; you can also let the AI know what they should feel like.

# 13  Specify the Desired Tone/Mood

"May I please ask you to be a little quieter? I need to focus on my work" and "Shut the f*** up! Your annoying jabbering keeps me from working" is substantially almost the same message. Yet they will likely be received very differently. (Just be polite! It will make your life much easier in general, and it will keep your blood pressure low.)

Do not just tell the AI *what* it should generate, but also *how* it should create it. An email may be written casually or in a formal tone. An image of a doll on a park bench may look peaceful or creepy. And a piece of music may sound happy or sad.

Here is a short list of words to give you a few first ideas on how you could describe your desired tone or mood. They will vary in suitability depending on the output medium.

- Cheerful
- Somber
- Aggressive
- Peaceful
- Witty
- Thought-Provoking
- Informal / Casual
- Formal / Professional
- Academic
- ...

Some services even allow you to prime their AIs with up-loaded material. For instance, you can have the AI produce outputs more in line with your corporate wording or your corporate design this way.

Some AIs may also have internalized the writing styles of particular authors or the art styles of specific painters. This way, you could easily have a birthday card painted by Vincent van Gogh and written by William Shakespeare.

While most people will consider the previous example un-problematic, I do not recommend directly copying the style of living artists. There is still quite a lot of legal debate on the implications of copyright law on any kind of generative art – I will touch on that later. But regardless of the out-come in future jurisdiction, I feel like paying living artists is just the right thing to do if you want art in their style.

# 14 Experiment with Phrasing

There are many ways to say the same thing. If your initial tries do not yield the desired results, try to phrase your prompt differently. There is a chance that the AI does not interpret the terms you used in your prompts the way you intended.

Try to figure out which part of the prompt is not functioning correctly, and then try to find synonyms for the respective words or paraphrase them. If you want the AI to depict "a street filled with cars," the AI might believe that you wish for vehicles piled above each other until the entire space between the houses on each side is filled. You might then rephrase this as "a street with a lot of cars." But "a lot" could also mean "a parking lot." So, the AI might generate an empty street with a parking lot next to it. Next, you might try your luck with "a traffic jam." The AI probably won't turn the cars into marmalade. But who knows? In this example, ambiguity might again become a problem. If you haven't already, make sure to read the chapter about avoiding ambiguity.

But in the end, it comes down to what was included in the training data of the respective AI model. One AI may have learned more about the meaning behind a particular word while it has less data about its synonym. If you are unlucky and use the more unfamiliar of those two words, you might end up thinking that the AI is not capable of fulfilling the prompt, while all it needed was a little rephrasing. So, switch up words to see if it improves the quality of your output.

Something very large is enormous. A Pegasus is a horse with wings. A feline with headgear is the same as a cat with a hat. If one way of wording does not work for you, try another one.

# 15 Get Inspiration

"Good artists copy, great artists steal." This quote is attributed to Pablo Picasso. It suggests that creativity cannot exist without helping oneself to the ideas of others. Considering that we all are influenced in our thinking by the cultural environment we live in, which in turn has been shaped by the ideas of those who came before us, it is difficult to refuse this notion altogether.

But if you ask me, there is a difference between drawing inspiration versus simply copying or stealing. So, please do not understand this part as a call for theft of intellectual property. Instead, consider it as a way of learning from the masters and to get inspired.

There are many websites and online communities in which users share their prompts and their outputs. Also, an increasing number of YouTube channels talk about impressive things they have been able to achieve with artificial intelligence. And some AI tools might even offer a public feed of their users' generated content together with the prompts they used to get those results.

If you are just starting out on your AI journey, it might be a good idea to go through these feeds and check out the prompts of the outputs you particularly like. It might teach you a lot about how to phrase prompts for a specific AI and help you understand how to describe certain styles better. Just don't simply copy others' prompts.

Furthermore, some AIs may allow you to reverse engineer a prompt, which could have been used to generate a particular result. In this case, you input the output, and the AI will write a fitting prompt. This does not only work with actual AI outputs, however.

Let's say you have a specific style of photography that you use on your website to give it a coherent look. If you need more photos with the same looks but a photo shoot would take too much effort, you could load one of your previous photos into a suitable AI and have it describe the image. This description will usually not only contain information about the pictorial object but also details about the photo's style. You can repeat this process with other images in your favored style and use the AI's descriptions to guide your prompts to have the AI generate more photos with the same looks.

But the realm of AI is not the only source of inspiration you can tap into for your prompts. Often your everyday life can be more inspiring than anything else and give you great ideas for what to generate next.

If you don't feel inspired by your day-to-day life, don't worry. This is something you can train. Try to challenge yourself: whenever you see something in real life you particularly like, try to ask yourself how you could recreate it digitally by working with AI. Over time you will begin to consider AI solutions to real-life problems automatically.

This is not to say that you should rely on AI for everything. At the time of writing this, most things are still better handled without AI. But expanding your tool belt to include potential AI-based approaches is a great practice. After all, the best solution is only of any help if it comes to your mind when needed.

# 16  Iterate

Think of your prompt as the guardrails to guide the AI in its output. Within these designated boundaries, however, the result can be understood as somewhat random. This opens up three approaches to getting as close as possible to your desired outcome:

**1) Repeat:**

If you are not content with the AI's output on the first try, you might want to have it rerun with the same prompt. Depending on how much or little your prompt narrows down what you want the AI to create, you might get somewhat different results the next time.

For example, if you ask an AI to generate an image of a cat without specifying anything about its style, you might get a photo, a children's drawing, or a Renaissance painting.

If your prompt is not completely off and the AI is, at least in theory, capable of creating the output you want, you should hypothetically get very close to your desired result if you have the AI work on the same prompt over and over again.

But since it is pretty much random, which kind of output the AI generates within the boundaries set by your prompt, there is no way of telling how many repeats it would take to end up with what you actually want. You might be sending the same prompt for hours, days, or even weeks before getting what you intended.

Thus, this method isn't efficient at all. I would only recommend running the same prompt repeatedly if the first output was already pretty close to what you had in mind, and you only need some minor variations to push it even closer.

**2) Adjust:**

Instead of repeatedly trying your luck with the same prompt, it's usually a better idea to modify your prompt based on previous results. Determine which parts of the prompt might lead the AI in the wrong direction, which information might be missing, and how you could rephrase your prompt to be even more specific.

This takes quite a bit of trial and error. The more experience you have with prompting, however, the closer your first attempt will get you to realizing your vision, and the fewer iterations you will need until you are satisfied with the result. But there will always remain a certain degree of experimentation.

And experimentation is the key here. Simply put, in scientific experiments, you compare separate groups regarding a particular outcome. Usually, you conduct these experiments to find causalities, to find out which intentionally induced variation within the test groups results in which other differences between these groups. A vital principle of these experiments is that you only change one aspect of these groups as a potential variable of influence at a time. Otherwise, the results become confounded.

Oftentimes this is easier said than done. Let's say you want to find out whether violent video games make their players aggressive. You might consider having one group of test subjects play violent video games while the other group just sits around. Then you measure each group's average level of aggression. Sounds like a well-thought-out experimental setting? Well, it isn't. In this case, you would not know whether it was, in fact, the violent video game that caused a potential difference in aggression. It could also be that doing anything makes people more aggressive than doing nothing (or vice versa).

(On a side note: way too many of the most polarizing studies cited by populist politicians suffer from this type of shortcoming. This is absolutely not to say that you should not trust scientists – quite the contrary. Bad studies get discussed and ripped apart by the scientific community all the time and, in most cases, don't even make it into peer-reviewed publications. But that usually does not make for great headlines.)

So why am I talking about scientific experiments this extensively? Because you should approach modifying your prompts in the same way. If you change multiple aspects of your prompt simultaneously, you won't know which adjustment caused which change in the results. So, unless your output is still extremely far off, you should only modify a single thing about your prompt at a time and see which effect this has on the output.

If you see that a change moves the output in the right direction, keep it. If it changes the results for the worse, however, keep working on this specific aspect of your prompt. Over time this will allow you to get closer and closer to your desired output. Plus, you will learn a lot about prompting along the way.

### 3) Improve:

Once you have generated an output close to what you anticipated, you might want to keep working on it. Many AIs allow you to use existing outputs as a basis of creating variations of them or to improve them in a certain way, specified by another prompt.

Whenever you prefer one of the new outputs over the prior, feed this new one back into the AI to keep improving on it. With each iteration, you should get gradually closer to the output of your dreams.

Some AIs also allow you to specify certain aspects of the output that you would like to improve. This includes features like inpainting and outpainting.

# 17  Be Patient

If the processes of repeating, adjusting, and improving sound lengthy to you, you are not mistaken. Depending on your ambition and your skills, it may take some time before you get what you want. So, patience is the key to getting the best results possible.

Also, practice makes perfect. Don't expect to write the most brilliant prompts the very first time you use a new AI. Prompting is just another skill you need to practice to master it. And the more proficient you become at prompting, the faster you will be able to create what you want.

The AI space tends to develop so rapidly that it is easy to feel like you cannot keep pace, like you are getting left behind. Even though I work with artificial intelligence almost every single day and constantly try out new things, I know this feeling myself too well. It would be a full-time job to keep up with all new developments in AI. And even then, you would have to work overtime and burn out.

But even though it may not feel like it, as long as you start working with AI on a regular basis, time is on your side. With every prompt you write and every output you generate, you will gain more experience. Plus, AIs are constantly improving, too. Within a few months, you will be able to get way better results than right now. You just have to be patient with yourself and the still-developing technology.

# 18  Save Prompts

Once you have found a prompt that works well for you, make sure to copy it and save it for later. I would suggest using Notion for this, which can be accessed via apps for Android, iOS, and Windows or directly through the browser of your choice. This makes it easy to access your prompt collection at all times from any device. But you could also simply paste your prompts into a text document and save it on your computer. Just find a way that fits best into your workflow.

Regardless of how you do it, saving well-performing prompts for later use is extremely valuable. This will save you a lot of time when you want to prompt the AI to do a similar task, especially since more complex prompts can become pretty expansive rather quickly.

Let's say you want the AI to write a blog post for your company every week. If you start from scratch to explain to the AI what your company does, who the intended target audience is, and what you want to achieve with the text every single time, you might as well write the entire blog post yourself. It would not take much longer.

The main reason why AI can be such a time saver is that it allows you to automate reoccurring tasks. As lined out before, optimizing prompts can be quite a lengthy process if you want to receive the best results. Thus, you can save more time if you do not have to repeat this process over and over again.

If you have a library of prompts that work well for your use cases, you can simply copy-paste them and substitute the parts that have changed for your current task.

# 19 Include Placeholders

What makes it even easier to adapt saved prompts to a new scenario is using placeholders. Think of placeholders as variables, which may contain any number or text. When working with placeholders, it is crucial to make it easy for the AI to recognize which parts of your prompt are meant to be placeholders. If an AI comes with a dedicated placeholder feature, you should, of course, define and implement the placeholders in the way intended by the AI's creators.

In all other cases, I like to put placeholders in square brackets because these symbols are otherwise hardly ever used in my prompts. Also, they are an easy way of defining the beginning and the end of a placeholder's name. This is very helpful when I want a placeholder name to consist of two words. Here is a very brief and simplified example of how I work with placeholders when prompting text-generating AI:

> [text genre] = blog post
> [text length] = 300 words
> [topic] = the top 10 most exciting destinations in Europe
>
> Write a [text genre] of around [text length] about [topic].

This example is extremely basic and short. When working with such short prompts, the benefit of using placeholders is marginal, if existent at all. But once your prompts start becoming more and more complex, this might save you quite a bit of time on repetitive tasks – if you store your prompts in a way that lets you quickly find them again whenever you need them.

While not all AIs understand when you include placeholder variables in your prompts, for those that do, this technique can be a true game-changer. This allows for even faster adjustment, as you do not have to go through the whole prompt to make adjustments but only have to change the values of the placeholder variables.

Furthermore, this even allows you to run a task multiple times at once with different sets of placeholder values by sending a single prompt. You would then have to tell the AI to execute the job again for each set of placeholder values you have defined before until it is done with all of them.

# 20 Look into Privacy Settings

You probably wouldn't stand in front of your competitors' offices, shouting your corporate secrets at them. So, you should not do this in the AI space either.

Some AIs use your prompts as data to further train their models. This means that if you paste the list of ingredients of your Krabby Patty into the prompt for an AI, Plankton would not have to hassle SpongeBob and his friends by trying to steal the recipe from them to learn about the fabled secret ingredient. He might simply be able to ask the same AI about it.

It probably goes without saying, but you should also value other people's privacy and never feed any AI with sensitive information about others without their explicit consent.

The information about whether an AI uses your prompts for further training is usually pretty well-hidden in the respective AI tool's Terms of Service. This can be a rather dry read. But if the AI is popular enough, you will probably find quite a few blog posts regarding the (lack of) privacy for your prompts.

Other AIs might share your outputs. For example, some image-generating AIs have public feeds showing off the creations of their users, sometimes including the prompt. This may be problematic for many reasons.

If you generate images to print on products, other users might steal them from the public feed and use them in the same industry. Depending on your jurisdiction, this might even be legal, as in some countries, AI-generated images are not protected by copyright at the time of writing.

Or, if you are an aspiring AI artist and have spent days, weeks, or even months finding your personal – reliably re-producible – art style, you probably don't want other artists to get too "inspired" by reading your prompts.

If you want to create a funny caricature of your boss, you probably don't want it to be publicly available on the inter-net with your profile pic right next to it. (Once again: re-spect other people's privacy. Do not casually load photos of others into an AI without their consent – even if it's your obnoxious superior!)

And last but not least, if you are using artificial intelligence to create marketing material for your new product, you might not want it to leak early on the internet before you have even launched the campaign.

The good news is, many AIs have some kind of privacy or stealth mode, which allows you to keep your prompts and your outputs to yourself. However, they usually come with a tradeoff of some kind. Some AIs might charge you extra for the privilege of privacy. Others might not save your prompts and outputs for later use by yourself while privacy mode is activated.

It is up to you to decide whether you want to activate privacy mode or not. But at the very least, you should keep in mind that privacy is something to consider while working with AI.

# 21  See if There Is an API

Now we are getting pretty advanced, but I'll try to explain it as simply as possible. All software consists of code in one form or another. Different applications may have been coded in different programming languages, and they most certainly use different parameters and functions. As a result, by default, separate applications cannot communicate with each other.

Developers may, however, decide to open their application to other pieces of software by implementing an API (short for Application Programming Interface). This API works as a bridge to connect the other pieces of software to the application. It usually consists of a couple of predefined lines of code that other developers can utilize in their programming to access specific features of the application behind the API.

In case you think that this does not matter to you because you are not going to code any applications yourself, you are only semi-correct. While you indeed don't need to know *how* an API works if you don't want to dive into coding, it is still good to know *whether* an AI does have an API. Because in this case, other applications may have already been docked to the AI – applications that might make your life easier.

Suppose your workflow revolves around taking the output from one application and using it in a prompt for an AI tool or vice versa. In that case, a connection may already exist between both applications, which automates this process for you. And even if there isn't, you might be able to build such a bridge without needing any coding skills by using automation tools, which serve as adapters between the APIs of hundreds, if not thousands, of applications.

And, of course, if you are a skilled developer yourself, the API opens even more possibilities to you. You might even consider developing and selling an application that dramatically improves the workflow of other users of an AI tool, and thereby profit from the AI hype without the need to dabble in AI model training yourself.

# Text-AI-Specific Advice

# 22  Ask the AI to Take on a Specific Persona

Do you want to write a speech in the style of Donald Trump? Do you need lyrics to a new rap song inspired by the style of Eminem? Or would you like to politely ask a bothersome salesman to f*** off in the style of William Shakespeare? All of this is easily possible with text-generating AIs. All you have to do is to ask the AI to assume the role of a specific person.

Be aware: in many cases, this will not only alter the output's style of speech but may also change its contents; Donald Trump would most likely talk about other things than William Shakespeare.

This might sound like a funny way of using text-generating AI – and it is. But there is also a dark side to it, as this technology can easily be abused for malicious intents, as it makes it easier to impersonate celebrities online. Please be very careful when someone contacts you on social media and claims to be a famous person. In most cases, they are scammers who are after your money or your login credentials.

Also, this raises ethical questions, even if it is only used for a giggle: is it okay to have an AI write a text in the tone of a specific person without their consent?

Either way, there is an even more interesting use case for specifying personas: have the AI take on the role of an expert in the field you would like the AI to help you with.

66

If you need a marketing strategy for your business, you would not just ask a random Joe on the street but instead consult a marketing specialist. If you need a well-written blog post, you would rather commission a copywriter than your cousin's seven-year-old son. And if you want advice on search engine optimization, you would contact an SEO expert instead of your gardener.

Everyone has a different set of skills. And since the AI could assume the role of anyone, you can tap into the specialized knowledge of every industry. Just let the AI know who you would like it to be.

As for a less serious use case: this can also be used to play games with the AI. For instance, I once wrote a rather lengthy prompt which asked the AI to take on the role of a storyteller and quest-giver. The AI should generate a fantasy adventure for me to experience as the story's hero. Every now and then, the AI should pause and give me a quest at a location within a radius of a hundred kilometers around my current position to fulfill in real life. The tasks were woven into the story. And only if I finished the quests would the story proceed. This was quite a unique experience. It truly felt like I was living an epic adventure and led me to see sights I otherwise probably never would have visited.

# 23 Define Unfamiliar Terms

Not all information is publicly available. Imagine you have recently invented the all new ingenious "Turbomaster 3000" and ask an AI to write marketing texts about your product for your yet-to-be-created website. The AI won't know whether the Turbomaster 3000 is a new vacuum cleaner for your bellybutton, a razor for shaving your cat, or a powerful hair dryer that uses a jet engine to evaporate all moisture (and probably also your skull) within seconds.

This does not mean that artificial intelligence cannot help you here, though. You just have to let the AI know what the Turbomaster 3000 actually is. Once you have taught the AI about the Turbomaster's incredible features, the intended target audience, and what makes it stand out from the competition, it will create excellent texts for you that will make everyone pull out their credit cards immediately to place an order.

This not only applies to product or brand names but also to personal names. Do you mean Donald Trump, the former president of the United States, who paid hush money to a porn star, or Donald Trump, the oncologist from northern Virginia? If you want the AI to write about the latter, you should explicitly tell the AI whom you mean, especially when you need a text about a person who is not all that well-known, you should always give the AI all of the information it might need to start writing.

On top of that, not all AIs have unrestricted access to the internet that would allow them to freely search for new information. Thus, they are restricted to the knowledge contained within their training data.

If an AI had been trained with information up to the middle of 2019, it would not have heard of the coronavirus pandemic at the beginning of the 2020s. It would have as little knowledge about COVID-19 as it has about the Turbomaster 3000.

However, it would have learned about other pandemics and know what a coronavirus is. If you feed all necessary information about this recent pandemic to the AI, it would still be able to interpret the new information in light of its prior knowledge and write coherent texts.

So, make sure you define all terms that might be unclear to the AI and double-check whether the outputs are factual. This should be common practice anyways but is especially important when working with words the AI might not be familiar with.

If you are unsure whether the AI has background knowledge about a specific term, you can simply ask the AI to define it for you. Should the AI give you a wrong definition, it is likely that the AI lacks information about said term and just made up a few facts to fulfill your request.

# 24  Give Context

Don't just tell the AI *what* you want it to do for you but also tell it *why* you need the respective output. As pointed out before, while the AI is very knowledgeable, there are simply things the AI cannot know about. This does not only apply to unfamiliar terms but also to your personal situation. The better the AI understands your needs, the better it can tailor its outputs to your specific case. I have witnessed time and time again that this can make the difference between a good and a great prompt.

If you would like the AI to write a text for your company, tell it more about your business situation. What kind of business do you have? Is it an established corporation, or is it a newly founded startup? What kind of product or service do you offer? Do you need the text to create awareness, or do you want it to convert already-interested people into paying customers? Who is your intended target audience for this specific text? Do you have a document outlining your corporate wording (the way your company speaks) that you could share with the AI?

You might even go so far as to share the results of your own data analysis with the AI. For instance, if you know which texts performed exceptionally well (and which didn't) in the past, you can copy these texts with the related data into your prompt and let the AI learn what works for your specific business and what doesn't. (But before you share any potential company secrets, you will want to read the chapter about privacy settings.)

Make sure to question everything you would consider to be evident. It certainly is obvious to you, but you probably know more about your situation than anyone else. And the AI will only know, in this regard, what you share with it.

# 25 Define a Target Audience

I already briefly touched on the fact that it helps to let the AI know which audience you are trying to reach with your text. Let me go a bit more into detail about why this is important and how to do it.

If you want the AI to write a marketing text for you, the AI might be able to guess your target audience from your type of product or service, or from the topic of your text. But in many cases, the same product or service can be relevant to many different target groups. By not telling the AI about your target audience, you risk getting an approximation of a one-size-fits-all solution, which will probably end up being far behind its potential in captivating any specific target group.

But there are also cases in which the AI might be misguided and guess completely wrong. If you want to give a talk about the main reasons for divorce, it makes a tremendous difference if you wish to present it to an auditorium at a sociology conference or to your partner.

Letting the AI guess your target audience may especially become a problem when you take an existing product and try to market it to an entirely new group to access a new market.

Imagine you would like to create and sell coloring books. Who would you sell them to? If children were your first idea, you are not wrong. Traditionally, coloring books are predominantly marketed to kids (and their parents, who will need to pay for them). However, in recent years, a whole new segment of coloring books has emerged that explicitly tries to appeal to adults. For this target group, fun and excitement are not the type of experience they seek from this product. They also probably don't need these books to train their hand-eye coordination. Much rather, they use the relaxing and meditative act of coloring predefined shapes as a means of unwinding after a stressful day. Accordingly, a marketing text optimized for getting parents to buy these books for their children can be remarkably counterproductive when trying to get adults to buy coloring books for themselves.

If you have any research data of your own on your target group, consider sharing it with the AI. Since this data is probably not publicly available, the AI would have no other way of knowing your insights. However, consider the points made in the chapter about privacy settings, as you probably want to avoid granting your competitors access to this type of data by training the AI model on your input.

As a quick side note: if you have raw data in a table format and want to share it with an AI that does not allow you to paste a table into the prompt input field, there may be a workaround. The CSV file format saves table data as a text file. Specific characters like commas, semicolons, or tab stops indicate the table's structure in this case.

So, open your table, (ideally after deleting all unnecessary information,) export its contents as a CSV file, open this file with a text editor of your choice, and copy all the content over to your prompt. If you are telling the AI that you are going to share table data in a CSV format, it may be able to interpret the data in the originally intended way.

Make sure to test whether the AI did, in fact, understand the structure of the data by asking the AI questions about the data, which you can easily verify. Depending on the AI, you may also be able to ask it to reproduce the data as a table. Some AIs can analyze the data for you. However, I would not rely on the results without checking for plausibility at the time of writing. With this workaround, you may give the AI access to your data even if it does not have a dedicated table import.

But of course, knowing your target audience is not only helpful in business contexts. If, for instance, you would like the AI to write a speech for a birthday party, it makes a huge difference whether it's your eight-year-old son's or your eighty-year-old grandfather's celebration, as the guests, their interests, and attention spans will likely differ accordingly.

Equally important for the AI to know is the situation in which you plan to reach your target audience. While a potential new customer might like to read about every single technical detail of your amazing product when they visit the product page on your website, you would bore them beyond imagination with exhaustive technical data when your Tik-Tok ad gets washed into their feed. And if you are trying to reach potential employees, a LinkedIn post and a Super-bowl ad should convey a different level of excitement.

The same target audience needs to be addressed differently in different situations. So, include this information in your prompt.

# 26 Ask the AI to Ask You Back

Have you ever listened to a toddler trying to tell a story? Often, they sound somewhat incoherent. This is mainly because young children cannot put themselves into other people's shoes. They struggle to realize what the listener cannot know, leaving out important parts of the story. At the age of around four years, an area of their brain is developed far enough to allow them to assume the perspective of others.

If you are reading this, you are likely much older than four. But even as adults, we are sometimes faced with the same problem: the more we concern ourselves with a certain topic, the more we believe the things we know about this field to be common knowledge. As a result, we don't feel the need to communicate these things explicitly. Furthermore, we might simply forget to mention important details.

All of this also applies to prompting AIs. To put it simply: you don't know what you don't know that the AI should know.

As discussed before, this can lead to problems when the AI lacks the information it should have to fulfill your request adequately. But there is a relatively easy fix when working with AI in a conversational chat setting. You can ask the AI to come up with questions to ask you to receive more information, which may help the AI do a better job at the actual task. Just like any freelancer you commission to do something for you would ask questions when they realize that your briefing lacks relevant information, you should give the AI the same opportunity.

Here's a little life hack for you: if you are giving a presentation and actually want your listeners to ask you their questions, do not ask, "Do you have any questions?" This allows them to simply shake their head and be done with it. People can be shy (and sometimes lazy) in social situations. It's better to ask, "What questions do you have?"

Apply the same trick to AI if you want it to ask you for more information. Directly prompt the AI to ask you questions to find out more background information, which will help it generate better outputs for the actual task later.

# 27 Have the AI Write and Improve Its Own Prompt

Do you still feel like you don't get what you wanted from your prompt? Why don't you let the AI improve your prompt for you?

You can take the advice from the previous chapter a step further: roughly describe what you need, ask the AI to come up with a suitable prompt and to ask you questions for more information, and to then improve the prompt based on your answers.

In this case, it is essential to define an iterative system of back and forth for the AI to follow to avoid any confusion. So, you will want to instruct the AI to always respond with a single refined prompt based on your prior answers and a new question to get more information and further improve the prompt. This way, you can always check how far the prompt has already been refined so that you know when to stop answering the AI's questions and when to start actually using the prompt.

This is immensely useful when you are working with AI to help you in a field you are rather unfamiliar with. Let's say you want the AI to write a contract for you but have no legal background. Or you need the AI to write code for you in a programming language you are unfamiliar with. Since, in these cases, you don't have the expertise to know which information the AI would require to create your desired output, it's a great idea to let the AI guide you.

But be careful with relying too much on artificial intelligence when the quality of the outputs is extremely important. AI does not (yet) fully replace a skilled lawyer or programmer, as the AI might not consider potential loopholes in your contract or might ignore critical security issues in your code, leaving the gate wide open for future hacking attempts.

# 28 Structure Your Prompts

When prompts become more complex, like in the previous piece of advice, their clarity and conciseness may suffer, but there is a relatively simple trick to keep your prompt from getting confusing for the AI: make sure your prompt is well-structured. So, subdivide your prompt into separate paragraphs, each following a coherent train of thought, building upon each other.

If your prompt becomes very lengthy, preface it with an overview of the structure of your prompt. This helps the AI understand which information to find where within your prompt. Also include information on how the AI should handle the information in each paragraph. Is it just background information to help the AI understand your needs? Or is it information the AI should actively weave into the output?

Some might have differing views on the practice of giving an overview first as it adds redundancy and clutter to your prompt. But I personally have seen the quality of my outputs increase when including such an overview in long prompts. As this is just anecdotal evidence, I would like to encourage you to test yourself whether your prompts do benefit from an outline or not.

The following pieces of advice will give you more detailed suggestions on how you could structure your prompts.

# 29  Start with a Synopsis of the Task

A friend of mine can talk for ages without getting anywhere. About ten to fifteen minutes in, she has often forgotten the point of her story. As an introvert, I do genuinely enjoy leaving the talking to her.

Still, it can be a little challenging to follow her meandering thoughts without yet knowing what point she is trying to make, especially when she goes far afield to explain the background of the story. When listening to her, I usually catch myself thinking more than once, *And why exactly are you telling me this?*

As outlined before, sometimes it is necessary to give context within a prompt for an AI to better understand what your prompt is about.

When your prompt gets longer, it may be beneficial to start off by giving the AI a quick summary of the actual task so that it knows what you want it to do with all of the context to guide its understanding of why the information you provide is relevant to the task at hand.

A few quick and short sentences like the following should be enough in most cases: "I would like you to write X about Y. But first, a bit of context..."

In this regard, the synopsis of the task is different to the overview of your prompt, which I talked about in the last chapter. While the overview is intended to introduce the AI to the structure of your prompt, the synopsis of the task prefaces all of this to give context to the context. This will guide the AI in its understanding of the purpose of all the additional information you provide.

# 30  End with a Request

Once you have provided the AI with all the information it could possibly need, you mustn't forget to finish off the prompt with a request – actually telling the AI what it should do for you. As this is easily the most essential part of your prompt and largely dictates the characteristics of the AI's outputs, you'll want it to be the last thing on the AI's mind. Thus, the actual request is best placed at the end of the prompt.

Try to be polite in your request. While at the time of writing this, AIs most likely are not self-aware yet, I do believe it is very likely that we will reach a point in time when we cannot rule out any longer that an AI has developed consciousness. So, I would recommend forming the habit of treating AIs with respect from the very beginning. This may sound like science fiction to you, and for now, it is. But many things that were first conceived by the minds of science fiction authors have become part of our daily reality. So, let's practice being nice – just in case.

# 31 Give Examples

If you have a very clear vision of what you would like the outputs to be like, you can give the AIs examples for outputs that would fulfill the requirements of your request.

You'll probably want to let the AI know that it should not simply replicate your example but come up with its own ideas that follow the example's model.

This is very helpful if you want the AI to create more of the kind of something you already have available or if it is rather complicated to describe what you want while it is easy to explain with an example.

But even in these cases, examples do not replace a proper prompt. The AI will still need to know what to do with the examples.

# 32  Be Objective

Each bias present in your prompt may translate into the output. This can be helpful when you are in a heated debate about what is the best kind of ice cream (walnut, of course!) and are running out of arguments. Then, you can ask the AI of your choice why walnut ice cream is the best.

But if you do not need artificial intelligence for ice-cream-related propaganda, you are better off with a more neutral output that reflects on arguments from all sides. This is especially important if you want to use the outputs to aid your decision-making.

Be very careful about this, as the AI may "hallucinate" facts. (This term is often used when artificial intelligence confidently talks about completely made-up stuff as if it was nothing but the truth.) On top of that, all misinformation present in the training data might be reproduced in the AI's outputs. Remember that a large portion of the training data was sourced from the internet. Just like you should not believe everything you read online, you should not mindlessly trust an AI, no matter how confident it seems in its reasoning.

But this also applies to many other use cases like brainstorming new ideas, writing informative blog posts, preparing news articles, or phrasing business emails.

While the creation of bias is rather evident in the previous ice cream example, a bias may also – subconsciously or deliberately – be introduced through framing. Using certain words may lock the AI into a particular viewpoint. Euphemisms are terms that have a positive connotation. Words, which invoke negative associations, are called dysphemisms. In many cases, euphemisms and dysphemisms exist to describe the same entity.

A group of rebels would consider themselves to be freedom fighters, while others might see them as terrorists. When people have died, you might say that they have departed or have finally kissed the dust. A protest for abortion rights may be framed as pro-choice or as legitimizing the murder of unborn children. Adult entertainment or obscene material can both be used as terms to describe pornography, in which people either make love or f**k. And companies can downsize (which is a euphemism itself) by either letting their employees go or by kicking them out.

Neither of these terms is correct or false in itself. They only take another perspective on the same subject. Depending on your worldview, beliefs, and experiences, you are more likely to use certain terms over others. This is not necessarily a problem. It's just important to be aware that some words may have a euphemistic connotation while others may be pejorative and that this can influence the perspective an AI takes when writing its outputs.

But a bias may also occur through context. If you first tell the AI about the importance of living out one's sexuality, the AI may be a bit more understanding towards sex offenders than if you first describe to the AI how much the victims of sexual violence suffer. By priming the AI to view the prompt in a specified context, you may influence its reasoning accordingly.

Again, this is not bad in itself as it offers another method of fine-tuning your prompts. But most importantly, you should know about this potential issue so that you don't induce any unwanted bias without even realizing it.

# 33 Avoid Rapid Topic Changes

Some AIs remember what was written before in the current session. They can and will consider your prior prompts and their previous responses in their following outputs. Thus, (unintentional) priming does not necessarily have to happen within a single prompt.

If you – completely out of the blue – come up with an entirely new topic, the AI will often try to interpret your new prompt in the context of the current conversation, leading to potentially awkward or nonsensical interactions.

So, if you have asked the AI before how to deal with a dog that refuses to listen to your commands and now you are asking the AI for instructions on how to grind meat, the AI might draw a rather sinister connection where there is none.

When working with AI tools, you should try your best to stick to a single topic per session. This will help the AI better understand what you are asking and provide more meaningful answers in return. If you change topics throughout a session, you should indicate this in your prompt, or even better, first reset the conversation to help the AI properly process your change in direction.

In the previous example, you might want to start an entirely new conversation with the AI or at least say something like, "Okay, let's start over and move to a different topic. Ignore our previous conversation when answering the following question: How do I grind meat?" This way, you give the AI a better chance at understanding your new prompt the way you intended and thus saves you time you would otherwise have to spend going through and ironing out potentially nonsensical outputs.

# Image-AI-Specific Advice

# 34 Layer Your Prompt

When prompting an image-generating AI to create a picture for you, use different layers to describe various aspects of your envisioned output in descending order of importance for the overall result.

Think of this like commissioning a human artist to create the image for you. First, they would need to know whether they should bring their camera or their canvas stand. Next, they have to understand what you want them to depict, then they would try their best to pose the pictorial object in the way you intended, and only then they would begin to adjust their camera settings or to mix and blend colors on their palette.

I personally have had a good experience with writing layered prompts in this structure:

*A [type of image] of a [pictorial object] [doing action], [style-defining attributes], [additional parameters].*

Of course, you should replace the parts in square brackets with the respective descriptions of your vision for the image.

Here are a couple of ideas on what types of images you could generate with AI:

- Professional Photo
- Children's Drawing
- Impressionist Painting
- Concept Art
- Character Design
- Line Art
- Digital Painting
- Website Design
- Doodle
- 3D Rendering
- Flat Design Artwork
- Product Design
- ...

The following pieces of advice will give you some ideas to fill in the slot for style-defining attributes in the example prompt structure above.

# 35 Use a Lot of Adjectives

Nouns are used to specify *what* should be in the generated image, and adjectives define *how* those entities should be implemented. Generally speaking, adjectives are used to express attributes of nouns. Thus, you can use adjectives to specify the characteristics of pictorial objects, e.g., *cute*, *brown*, or *happy*, to further describe a cat's appearance. But you can also implement adjectives in your prompts to describe the overall look of the image, such as *cinematic*, *geometric*, or *peaceful*.

The more adjectives you incorporate into your prompt, the more information you can provide to the AI on what you want the resulting output to look like. In fact, adjectives are usually what give you the most control over the looks of the generated images. From my experience, prompts that contain more adjectives produce more interesting results. Of course, this is not to say that you should spam random adjectives into your prompt. Only use words that make sense in describing your vision.

# 36 Specify Colors

If you want to generate images for a specific use case, some colors will likely be more fitting than others. So far, I have often given examples in the context of business, so let's look at a private scenario this time. Let's say you want a new artwork to hang on the wall of your bedroom and decide to have it generated by AI. Being a perfectionistic interior designer, you have already meticulously fine-tuned the colors of your wall paint, the carpet, the curtains, and your bed sheets to match each other perfectly.

Of course, you would want the new art piece to fit into this ensemble – either by matching the color of the other elements or by purposefully using complementary colors to make it stand out as a true eye-catcher. Either way, you certainly would not leave the colors of the output to chance. Instead, you'd want to tell the AI precisely which colors you desire to be in the final art piece. You achieve this by incorporating the names of the exact color(s) you are looking for into your prompt – do you want crimson or ruby-red? This will give you a lot of control over the resulting colors.

But there are also other ways you can define colors. Oftentimes you do not care which exact colors are being used by the AI to create the final output. Instead, you want to create a specific look or atmosphere. Here are a few ideas for words that might help you describe the colors you have in mind:

- Bright
- Dark
- Saturated
- Muted
- Monochrome
- Warm
- Cold
- Neon
- Vibrant
- Vivid
- Pastel
- Intense
- Cinematic
- ...

This way of describing colors is especially helpful if you want the depicted objects to still retain their original color variations in relation to each other. In the light of a sunset, all things will have a warm golden tint, yet the leaves of a tree will still look a bit more greenish compared to its trunk.

If you want to go really artsy, you can even look up the metaphorical meanings associated with each color to help convey a message with your generated artwork But beware: the meanings of colors may vary between different cultures.

# 37 Learn the Vocabulary of an Artist

The colors of an output are only one of many features defining an image. A painter uses the strokes of their brush to create beautiful pieces of art. As a generative artist, you are painting with your words. What will help you a lot with this is learning the vocabulary of an artist. Knowing the right words, you will be able to describe more precisely what you want to create.

You could dedicate a whole book to all the different terms artists use to talk about the characteristics of their artworks, but I would like to give you at least a quick overview of the most essential aspects.

| Term | Meaning |
|------|---------|
| Brightness | The brightness of an image describes how much light there is in the picture. Is the image filled with darkness and shadows, or is it bright or even blinding? By tweaking the brightness of your creation, you can strongly influence the reception of the image. Darker images tend to invoke feelings of dread and sadness and look more mysterious, while brighter images feel more cheerful and welcoming. |

| | |
|---|---|
| Saturation | The saturation of an image defines the strength of the colors in your picture. A black-and-white image would be desaturated entirely, while a picture beaming with bright colors would be considered highly saturated. Images with a lower saturation usually look more serious and potentially a bit somber. A high saturation makes images look more cheerful but also potentially more childish. |
| Contrast | There are many different kinds of contrast. When people talk about contrast in images, they usually mean differences in brightness. Having a high contrast then implies that the dark parts of a picture are very dark, and the bright areas are especially bright. A high contrast in brightness is usually considered to look hard, tough, and bold, while a low contrast may look soft and weak. |
| | But there are also color contrasts. You might want to look into complementary contrasts. These are pairs of colors which are very different from each other, as they have opposing |

positions on the color wheel. Their combination is usually considered to be visually harmonic, like blue and orange or red and green.

You could also have contrasts in saturation. Think of a bright pink neon sign in a grey city environment.

Also, you can work with contrasting topics in an image. As an example, try to picture a kneeling child holding a beautiful flower amidst a war scene with fighting soldiers, explosions, and buildings in ruin.

| | |
|---|---|
| Sharpness | The sharpness of an image defines how crisp or blurry a picture looks. In most cases, a high level of sharpness will be what you are looking for. But in some cases, you might want to go for a softer or dreamier look. You might also want to generate a blurry background to put behind the photo of a person. |
| Depth of Field | The depth of field is related to sharpness. It specifies how far into the distance the background and foreground of a focused object remain sharp. A very narrow depth of field |

makes the foreground and background blurry, while an extremely large depth of field allows you to have everything crisp at once.

You may have already noticed visually pleasing bubbles of light in the blurry background of some photos. They are created in various shapes by using different lenses in photography. This phenomenon is called "bokeh" and can be easily summoned into your creations by using this term.

| Vignetting | A vignette is a gradual change in characteristics of the image towards its borders and especially its corners. Typically vignettes make the image darker the further you move away from its center. This often occurs naturally in photography, as some lenses let in less light toward the frame's borders. Because of this, we are very used to seeing a small amount of vignetting in photos. As a result, vignettes can make an image look more well-rounded and even more realistic to us. |

| | |
|---|---|
| Composition | The composition of an image describes the placement of its elements in relation to each other. The visual weight of pictorial objects and lines formed by the elements of the image play an important role when it comes to composition. Probably the most well-known composition rule is the golden ratio, which is considered to look very harmonic. If you are wondering, the golden ratio is at around 61.8% of the width and/or height of an image. |

This list is far from complete. There are many other concepts and terms to learn if you really want to prompt like a true artist, but this should give you a good starting point.

# 38 Have the AI Give Shape to the Abstract

What does the meaning of life look like? How do you depict emotions like happiness, anger, or sadness abstractly in creative artworks? Among the tens of thousands of images I have generated with AI, it was usually those trying to manifest abstract concepts that stood out the most to me. These images were usually more artistically interesting and thought-provoking than any attempts at realism.

While image-generating AIs become increasingly better at recreating all kinds of objects and living things, it is the AIs' ability to create images based on abstract concepts where their artistic skills truly shine. Plus, in the resulting pictures, slight imperfections do not matter at all as they can be considered creative freedom in a rather abstract and often surreal-looking piece of art.

Furthermore, finding existing stock images that express such shapeless concepts can be incredibly challenging. Stock images are pictures that were originally created without a specific use case in mind and are made available through large databases for anyone to use (after usually paying a license fee). They are often used in marketing, since having a photo shoot for every single image needed would be pretty pricy and take a lot longer than looking up a suitable photo online.

It does not take much effort to find a stock photo of a happy and excited person to use in your ads. But try to find a stock image precisely depicting weltschmerz (instead of just regular sadness). For these cases, image-generating AIs are especially helpful.

Granted, such pieces of art are not a perfect fit for any use. Suppose you want to generate images for a company with a relatively restrictive corporate design that only allows for the use of photographs. In that case, these artistic renditions of abstract concepts will most likely not be permitted for use by this company.

(On a side note: AI-generated images are here to stay. If a corporate design strictly prohibits the use of AI art, it might be time to consider adjusting these rules.)

# 39  Create the Nonexistent

Pictorial objects do not necessarily have to be abstract in order not to exist. Our mind has the amazing ability to come up with new things we have never seen in real life. Think of a giant eyeball floating above Tokyo, a tree with clocks instead of fruits, or a heart made of circuit boards.

Surreal ideas like this would make for exciting artwork. And once again, you would probably be out of luck trying to find these in stock image archives (though more and more AI-generated images find their way onto stock platforms).

As long as you describe it, AI will (in most cases) be able to generate it. However, I have to admit that AIs usually take more tries to get to what you imagined the crazier your ideas become. Try to use synonyms or different phrasing and reorganize the structure of your prompt until you are satisfied. If you haven't already, read the chapter "Experiment with Phrasing".

If the AI still struggles then, it might have problems understanding in which way it should combine the different objects in your image. In this case, you might want to use an AI that offers some inpainting capabilities so that you can create different pieces of the image separate from each other.

# 40 Work with Other AIs to Improve Your Images

Running AI models to create pictures takes a lot of computing power. While high image resolutions may be desirable regarding image quality and level of detail, they come with a trade-off. Images with a high resolution take much longer for the AI to finish. And since the number of pixels in an image is determined by its area, it grows much faster than you might assume. If you increase both the height and width of a picture by a factor of two, the number of pixels quadruples. Accordingly, the generation of larger images is much more demanding and slower.

To a certain degree, this could be accelerated by investing in more powerful hardware. But this again comes with a cost: the fastest GPUs (graphics processing units) are pricey and use more electricity for running and cooling. As a result, you can only pick two of these three: large resolution, fast generation, or inexpensive pricing.

As a solution to this dilemma, many image-generating AI services use a little trick: they first generate an image in a relatively small resolution and then, in a separate step, take this image and have an upscaling AI model guess what the pictorial information in between the existing pixels would look like if the picture had been created in high resolution to begin with.

But you do not have to stop there. Upscaling AIs are widely available in varying degrees of quality. While the most powerful AIs usually come with a price tag, there are also some reasonably capable free options. Upscaling images allows you to use them in use cases requiring a higher resolution because the pictures would otherwise look blurry or even pixelated if they had a lower resolution.

If you want to use your creations in a video, you will want to reach at least Full HD resolution (1920 x 1080 pixels for landscape orientation).

Also, if you want to have your images printed, the original output resolution is usually insufficient. The larger you want the resulting print to be and the smaller the distance from which people will look at the print, the larger the resolution should be. Since the required resolution largely depends on printing size, the requirements are usually specified in dpi (dots per inch – how many pixels fit into an inch of printing size).

If the image is mainly viewed at a close distance, like a postcard, you will want to have at least 300 dpi. For large posters, which will mostly be viewed from farther away, 150 dpi may also be sufficient. To find the necessary resolution for a crisp print, you take the required dpi as specified by the printing shop and multiply the value by the height and width of the desired printing format in inches. You might be surprised by how many pixels are actually required for a crisp print. If you divide the resulting target resolution by your current resolution, you will receive the factor by which you will need to upscale the image to obtain the print resolution.

If this was too much math for your taste, let's jump straight into an even more exciting topic: copyright law.

# 41 Reverse-Search Your Creations

Let me preface this chapter by saying that I am not a lawyer. So please take the following paragraphs with a pinch of salt.

Generative art and copyright have a rather complicated relationship. At the time of writing, there is a furious debate about whether AI companies should be allowed to train their models on publicly available images from the internet without even asking the creators.

While one side argues that using the images of artists without their permission to create a new product (by using them in the training data for an AI) constitutes a copyright infringement, the other side argues that training an AI is similar to how humans learn. To put it simply, the AI looks at a myriad of pictures of apples and oranges until it understands their defining features, learns to tell them apart, and can create new images of those fruits.

In my opinion, both sides make a valid point. I perfectly understand that artists are anything but delighted that, after taking years to perfect their craft, their works are being used for free to create a technology that threatens to replace them. But on the other hand, the proponents of AI technology are correct in that the influence of a single image among billions typically contained within training data is minuscule.

Furthermore, I am convinced that AI technology will advance to a point at which we will have discussions about

108

whether certain AI entities should receive the same rights as human beings, which would make it feel rather strange to ban them from such fundamental things as learning from publicly available sources in general or taking a look at certain images. (However, I believe discussions on AI rights won't last too long. Soon enough, at least one AI will reach capabilities that – from a human perspective – are more akin to those of a god than a human being, making it ridiculous to try to subject the AI to human law.)

And then there is also a discussion on whether the outputs of image-generating AIs can be protected by copyright. In many legislations, only creations by human beings can be subject to copyright.

What do AIs and monkeys have in common? They both aren't human. Have you heard of the macaque who took a selfie? Between 2011 and 2018, a series of disputes were brought to court concerning the question of whether the monkey who took the photo or the photographer who had created the situation, which allowed for the picture to be taken, should be legally considered the copyright owner of the photo.

In the end, a US court ruled that the monkey was the creator of the image. And since it was not a human being, it could not own any copyright. Thus, the photo was in the public domain and free to use for anyone.

There have also been court cases regarding AI. One of the very first cases was that of the comic *Zarya of the Dawn*, which was illustrated using Midjourney. In the eyes of the court, the illustrations were not created by the comic's author, Kris Kashtanova, but by a machine and thus are not copyrightable.

In my personal opinion, this black-and-white thinking won't withstand future developments. At the time of writing, AI is being incorporated into more and more features of established design tools like Photoshop. Even before text-to-image AI models were built into Photoshop, many features were already assisted by AI, like subject detection for background removal or retouching tools. So, at what point does the human artist stop being the creator?

If you ask me, as long as AIs cannot hold any copyright itself, the most important factor in determining whether a generated image should be protected by copyright law is how much human creativity went into its creation.

You can ask an AI to generate a random image of a cat. That is not very creative, and I agree that the resulting pictures should not be protected by copyright. However, there are generative artists who have spent months crafting and refining their own recognizable and reproducible style of AI art, then spent hours engineering the perfect prompt to make their idea become reality, and then went through countless iterations to find the one image that most closely matches their vision. I would argue that these artists should be considered the (co-)creators of the generated images, which in turn should be protected under copyright law.

But that is just my personal opinion. We will see how copyright law will adapt to this changing situation over the following years.

These digressions were meant to illustrate one thing: there are many discussions to be had about AI-generated creations and copyright. Regardless of the outcome of these discussions, it is essential to note that AI may (re)produce outputs that infringe on other people's or companies' rights, such as copyrights or trademarks, held by these entities.

A study by Carlini et al. (2023) found that in rare cases, diffusion models (a prominent type of image-generating AI models) recreated almost exact copies of the images they were initially trained on when being prompted with the original, verbatim caption of said images.

While this certainly is an edge case scenario, it cannot be completely ruled out that AI sometimes generates outputs that resemble copyrighted material. To me, this is no reason to refrain from using this kind of technology. After all, even human artists may accidentally create something similar to protected works.

Think of a composer who believes to have come up with an ingenious new melody just to be later sued by someone who had the same idea. The composer may or may not have heard the melodic theme subconsciously in the mall while shopping, and certainly, they did not intend to steal someone else's work, but this makes no difference in terms of copyright law. All that matters is the similarity of both melodies.

So, running into legal problems of this kind cannot be avoided entirely even when commissioning a human being to create something for you. I would expect the probability of accidentally reproducing copyrighted material to be lower the more detailed your prompt becomes. At a certain level of complexity, it is just highly unlikely that anyone has created something extremely similar before. Still, there is no guarantee.

There is a pretty easy way to mitigate these risks, however. You can reverse-search your generated images with Google's image search. If Google cannot find any strikingly similar pictures, it's pretty likely that there are none. I recommend always doing this when you intend to use generated images publicly and/or commercially. While there is no bulletproof protection from legal claims (especially unjustified ones), it's a good idea to play it as safe as possible.

Learning about legal risks may feel intimidating. However, quite the opposite should be the case – knowing about potential risks allows you to circumvent them. So, you should actually feel safer.

Needless to say, you should refrain from intentionally prompting the AI to generate images that contain the intellectual property of others. While it might be funny to create a hyper-realistic photo of Super Mario, Nintendo's lawyers would be well within their rights to go after you when you print it on shirts and sell it in your shop.

# Final Words

Now you have learned a lot about prompting, including many secret tricks of prompt engineers. This will allow you to write more powerful prompts than most other people. But as a wise man once said, "With great power comes great responsibility." This wise man was Spider-Man's uncle. So, please use your new powers responsibly and do good.

As I have outlined, this knowledge can be abused for malicious intents. Don't turn to the dark side. Instead, use your prompting skills to create value – not only for yourself, but also for the people around you.

While spamming, scamming, and the like may be tempting for quick short-term benefits, I sincerely believe that in the long term, you will always be better off playing fairly. It does not matter whether you believe in karma or a higher power. People will remember what you did to or for them – and they will prefer to work with, order from, and interact with someone who has treated them kindly.

## Things Will Change – Quickly

As mentioned before, we are very likely just witnessing the beginning of an exponential development in the realm of AI technology. As is the case with all exponential curves, retrospectively, the incline at the beginning always looks rather slow.

If you are already impressed by what AI can do today, you will most certainly be totally blown away by the capabilities of AI in the future.

These advancements in technology may also change the way we interact with AIs. While I tried my best to select information for this book that won't be obsolete tomorrow so that what you have learned should provide value for you over the course of the next few years, there might come a point in time at which particular pieces of advice might become outdated. So, please make sure to keep an eye out for new developments in the AI space.

Right now, no one knows where this journey will take us, but buckle up, because one thing is for sure: it will be quite an exciting ride.

Before you go, if this book has provided any value to you, it would mean the world to me if you could recommend it to a friend or give it an honest review. Thanks a lot for reading, and happy prompting!